Judy Moody's

Double-Rare Way-Not-Boring
Book of Fun Stuff to Do

Megan McDonald   illustrated by Peter H. Reynolds

CANDLEWICK PRESS
CAMBRIDGE, MASSACHUSETTS

Meet Judy Moody!

Name: Judy Moody

Address: 117 Croaker Road

Phone Number: 555-JUDY

School: Virginia Dare School

Teacher: Mr. Todd

Principal: Ms. Tuxedo

And now introduce yourself. . . .

Name: _____

Address: _____

Phone Number: _____

School: _____

Teacher: _____

Principal: _____

Knock-Knock

Knock-knock. *Who's there?*
Stink. *Stink who?*
Stink you'd know
your own little brother.

Knock-knock. *Who's there?*
Frank. *Frank who?*
Frank you for the
birthday present.

Knock-knock. *Who's there?*
Toad. *Toad who?*
Toad you to keep out
of my room!

Knock-knock. *Who's there?*
Hedda. *Hedda who?*
Hedda toad named
Toady, but I let him go.

JoKes!!

Knock-knock. *Who's there?*
Pencil. *Pencil who?*
Pencil-vania.

Knock-knock. *Who's there?*
Newt. *Newt who?*
Newt England is where
the American Revolution
started.

Now it's your turn!
Can you write some jokes
that will *knock-knock* your
socks off?

Knock-knock. *Who's there?*
Pasture. *Pasture who?*
Pasture bedtime, Stink!

Judy Moody Slang Dictionary

From *double rare* to *star-spangled bananas,* here's a look at some of Judy Moody's favorite expressions. With this Judy Moody slang dictionary, you'll never be at a loss for words — and that's definitely double cool!

rare!: cool!

double rare!: way cool!

double cool!: twice as cool!

ROAR!: what to say when you're angry or frustrated

pizza table: the little plastic piece that keeps a pizza from touching the top of the pizza box

bothers: little brothers who bother you all the time!

smad: sad and mad, at the same time!

same-same: what you say when you and your friend do something that's the same

phoney baloney: fake

not-boring: interesting

boing!: aha!

star-spangled bananas!: what you say when you're surprised or amazed

L.B.S.: Long Boring Story

Ouch Face: the face you make when someone's pulling your hair

ABC gum: Already Been Chewed gum

nark: bad mood

T. P. Club: the Toad Pee Club

oogley: gross

caterpillar eyebrow: the way your eyebrows look when you're in a mood (not a good mood, a bad mood!)

or something: what you say when someone presents you with a list of choices that end with "or something" and you don't agree with any of the choices

V.I.Q.: Very Important Question

Antarctica: the desk at the back of Mr. Todd's classroom where you have to sit if you're causing trouble

goopy: cheesy

Who's Who

Who's who in the Judy Moody world? Fill in the speech bubbles to show what you think Judy and her friends are saying. Use the slang dictionary to help you!

Judy
Queen of moods

Mom
Judy's mother

Stink
Judy's little *bother*

Dad
Judy's father

Mr. Todd
World's greatest
third-grade teacher

Rocky
Judy's best friend

Jessica
Know-it-all

Toady
Mascot of the T. P. Club

Frank
Used to eat paste

Who's Who in Your Life?

Draw or paste pictures of your family, friends, and pets in the circles below, and write your own mini-descriptions of each person below their picture. Don't forget to include yourself!

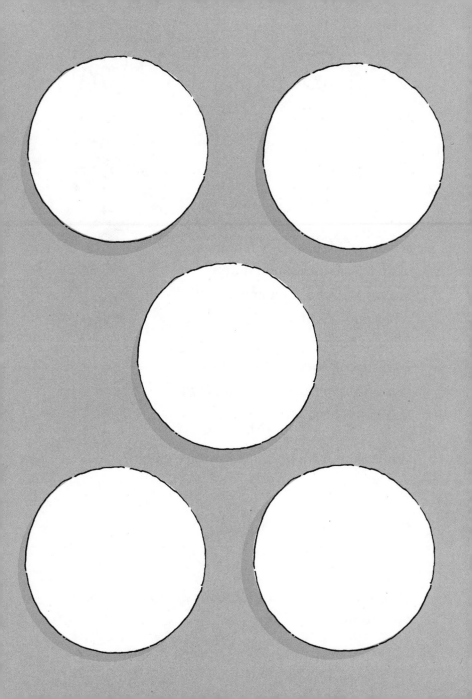

Be a Screamin' Mimi!

I scream
You scream
We all scream
FOR ICE CREAM!

Screamin' Mimi's is the real name of an ice-cream shop in author Megan McDonald's hometown of Sebastopol, California. Megan's favorite flavor is coffee ice cream with chocolate chips. Judy Moody's favorite flavors are Chocolate Mud and Rain Forest Mist.

What is your favorite flavor of ice cream?

What toppings do you like?

If you had your own ice-cream shop, what would you name it?

Did you know...

The idea for *Judy Moody Gets Famous!* came to Megan McDonald when she was at Screamin' Mimi's. She didn't want to forget her idea, so she wrote it down on a Screamin' Mimi's napkin!

Try it! Get a plain paper napkin and list some of YOUR ideas to write about.

Use the drawing at right to build your own ice-cream cone. Color it in to make it look "scooper" delicious. Use your favorite flavors as inspiration!

Top flavor: _____

Middle flavor: _____

Bottom flavor: _____

Here's a poem
all about Judy Moody,
and it spells her name.
It's called an
acrostic.

Jaws is her favorite pet.

Under her pillow is the dictionary.

Declares independence from brushing her hair.

Yuck! Member of the Toad Pee Club!

Moods, good and bad.

Or something!

Operates on a zucchini.

Dresses up as Elizabeth Blackwell, First Woman Doctor.

Yes, she really did eat a shark.

Spell YOUR name in an acrostic below,
and make up a poem all about YOU!

_____ _____

_____ _____

_____ _____

_____ _____

_____ _____

_____ _____

_____ _____

_____ _____

_____ _____

Collections

Judy and her friends love to collect things!

Judy collects:

pizza tables

scabs

toothpicks

Band-Aids

spare doll parts

baseball erasers

Frank collects:

marbles

rubber bugs

erasers

buffalo nickels

comic books

miniature soaps

How many items are in your best collection?

What's the most unusual collection you have?

Try starting a collection that's RARE. Some ideas are: books with mistakes, old stamps, old buttons, fossils, autographs, four-leaf clovers, coins that aren't round. . . .

Furry Friends

Here's a list of Judy's stuffed animals:

Ned Bear
Ted Bear
Fred Bear
Cornflake (not-cloned Guinea pig)
Brownie
Tookie (Toucan)
Snowflake (Loon from Minnesota)
Auggie
Doggie
Pepper (smells like pepper)

What stuffed animals do you have?

Are there any that have a special meaning?

Any you've had since you were a baby?

My Room

Judy's favorite spot to hang out is her top bunk. What's your favorite place to read, think, dream?

Here's what you might find under Judy Moody's bed:

- pizza tables
- a dried-up prune
- Mouse
- dust bunnies
- a lost sock

What's lurking in the dust under your bed?

Are you neat or messy?

Where do you fit on the scale below?

___ Neat freak   ___ Slightly disheveled

___ Neat enough   ~ cʰᴬºs!

In a messy mood? Clean it up!

- ⊚ Hang up a bulletin board where you can collect your notes, postcards, ticket stubs, and other stuff you want to save.

- ⊚ Give away something you don't need anymore to a friend.

- ⊚ Pick up ten things from the floor.

- ⊚ Decorate boxes to keep your stuff in.

In a party mood?

- Put up a string of fun lights, like chili peppers or sunflowers.

- Put your birthday cards on a string and hang it on the wall.

- Get a Mylar balloon and let it float to the ceiling.

- Hang paper streamers or a paper chain from the ceiling or around your bed.

In a nature mood?

- Collect some rocks, shells, or colored beach glass, leaves, acorns, or pinecones to display on your bookcase or windowsill.

- Decorate your window with paper snowflakes.

- Hang a crystal in your window and watch it make rainbows on the walls.

- Be a stargazer — stick glow-in-the-dark stars and planets to your ceiling.

Trace and cut out the doorknob hanger below to keep your "bothers" and sisters out of your room!

You can write your own message on the other side — be creative!

This room belongs to

_____

KEEP OUT!

(This means you, _____.)

Watch Out!

If you get too close to a volcano, you might catch:

PNEUMONOULTRAMICROSCOPICSILICOVOLCANOCONIOSIS
from breathing the volcano dust!

Wow! The longest word in the dictionary — not even Jessica Finch, Queen Bee, can spell that!

How many words can you make using only those 45 letters? A couple are listed below to get you started:

cranium

ultramarine

_____

_____

_____

_____

_____

_____

_____

_____

_____

_____

Now try doing the same with
ANTIDISESTABLISHMENTARIANISM
or with
HIPPOPOTOMONSTROSESQUIPEDALIAN.
(Find out what these words mean at the back of the book.)

Make a ME Collage!

You can draw or cut out pictures and paste things to your collage. Here are some ideas to get you started:

- Who I am
- Where I live
- My friends
- My best friend
- My favorite pet
- When I grow up . . .
- Hobbies

- Clubs
- The best thing that ever happened to me
- The worst thing that ever happened to me
- The funniest thing that ever happened to me

Write down your ideas here, but make your final collage on a separate piece of paper or poster board. Be creative! It's all about what makes you YOU.

Judy Moody

and her friends are part of a very special club: the T. P. Club.

Do you belong to any clubs?

Did you know that all of the clubs below are real?

- ❧ National Rhyming Names Club
- ❧ Left-Handers Club
- ❧ Rubber Ducky Fan Club
- ❧ Bubblegum Club

Invent your own club! What should it be called?

 Don't forget to go to www.judymoody.com
to join the Official Judy Moody Fan Club!

Record-Breaking Ideas

The members of the T. P. Club tried to break the world record for the longest human centipede. Here are some other crazy records — for real!

- If you're older than 6, it's too late to be the youngest world line-dance champion, but you still have time to become the youngest doctor (17 years old)!

- If you can get more than 72,000 people together, you can do the world's largest chicken dance!

- You can always just grow your toenails . . . but each one would have to be almost 9 inches long! Ewwww!

What record would you really like to break?

Can you think of a new record you'd like to set?

Judy Moody Gets Famous!

★ ★ ★ ★ ★ ★ ★ ★ ★ ★ ★ ★ ★

NEWS

She, Judy Moody, Phantom Doll Doctor, now felt as famous as Queen Elizabeth, as famous as George Washington, as famous as Superman. **FAMOUSER!**

Excerpt from *Judy Moody Gets Famous!*

Judy Moody finally gets her chance to be famous. What about you?

What would you like to be famous for? Draw or paste your picture on the front page of the newspaper on the next page and write your own headline above it. Now you can be in your family's **HALL OF FAME** — just like Judy!

★ ★ ★ ★ ★ ★ ★ ★ ★ ★ ★ ★ ★ ★

All About Pets

Give your pet a makeover!

Before

After

Draw or paste a picture of your pet below.

Now draw a funny outfit on him or her!

Do you have any pets?

If so, which is your favorite?

If not, what pet would you like to have?

What's your pet's greatest talent?
Add your pets to the chart below:

Judy

pet: Mouse

species: cat

talent: makes toast!

pet: Jaws

species: Venus flytrap

talent: eats hamburger

Stink

pet: Toady

species: toad

talent: initiates members
of the T. P. Club

Frank

pet: Sparky

species: dog

talent: jumps through
a Hula-Hoop

Rocky

pet: Houdini

species: iguana

talent: can lose his tail

Your pets

pet:

species:

talent:

pet:

species:

talent:

pet:

species:

talent:

Make a Difference!
Heal the World!

"I'm going to live up here now. Like Julia Butterfly Hill."

"Who?"

"The girl who lived in a tree for two years. Mr. Todd told us. They were going to cut down some ancient redwoods in California, so Julia Butterfly Hill climbed one of the trees and stayed there. They couldn't cut down a tree with a person in it. She even named the tree Luna."

"You can't just live in a tree, Judy," said Stink.

"Judy Monarch Moody to you."

Excerpt from *Judy Moody Saves the World!*

Save the Rain Forest!
Save the Animals! World Peace!
What will you do to change YOUR world?
How will YOU make a difference?

Choose one idea and do something about it.
Here are some ways to get started:

Make a sign.

Write a letter.

Start a petition. Get your
friends to sign it.

Put on a play to raise
awareness.

Have a sale to raise
money for your cause.

ENDANGERED!

Endangered species in Judy's home state of Virginia:

- **northeast beach tiger beetle**
- **Shenandoah salamander**
- **monkeyface mussel**
- **shiny pigtoe**
- **bald eagle**

Find out about endangered species in your home state. Make a list here:

_____

_____

_____

_____

_____

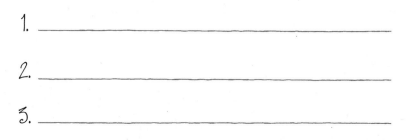

Find out three important fun facts about your
endangered species:

1. _____

2. _____

3. _____

Draw a picture of your endangered species:

Help Save the World!

Write about how you might try to save one of the
endangered species in your state:

_____

_____

_____

_____

_____

_____

_____

_____

_____

Endangered Species Word Match

Frank pointed to a beetle with a shiny green head and eyes like an alien. Printed below the beetle it said *Cicindela dorsalis dorsalis.*

"That's not a northeast beach tiger beetle," said Judy. "It's some kind of a Cinderella beetle."

"It's Latin," said Frank.

"Latin? Don't they have any beetles that speak English?"

Excerpt from *Judy Moody Saves the World!*

Can you match the scientific names of these endangered species to their common names? The first one is done for you. For the rest you might want to visit your library or look in some field guides! (Or check the answers at the back of the book.)

northeast beach tiger beetle   *Euphilotes battoides allyni*

El Segundo blue butterfly   *Fusconaia cor*

tooth cave spider   *Plethodon shenandoah*

shiny pigtoe   *Gambelia silus*

blunt-nosed leopard lizard   *Neoleptoneta myopica*

Shenandoah salamander   *Cicindela dorsalis dorsalis*

PENCIL-MANIA

Judy stopped chewing on her Grouchy pencil. She stared at it. The grouchy face looked even grouchier. This pencil used to be a tree. A rain forest tree!

She, Judy Moody, would never, ever use a pencil again.

Excerpt from *Judy Moody Saves the World!*

A few fun facts about pencils:

- One tree can make 172,000 pencils.
- One pencil can draw a line 35 miles long.
- One pencil can write 45,000 words!
- Benjamin Franklin advertised pencils for sale in his *Pennsylvania Gazette* in 1729.
- William Monroe, a cabinetmaker in Concord, Massachusetts, made the first American wood pencils in 1812.
- John Steinbeck wrote *The Grapes of Wrath* using as many as 60 cedar pencils every day!
- A pencil will write in zero gravity, upside down, and underwater!

- Seventy-five percent of the pencils sold in the United States are painted yellow! In the 1800s, this was to honor the Chinese and let people know that their pencils contained Chinese graphite — the best in the world!

- More than 2 billion pencils are used in the United States every year.

- Find out a fun fact about other school supplies. Check your library. Try an encyclopedia. Surf the Internet.

What can you find out about paper? Glue? Chalk? Erasers?

_____

_____

_____

_____

_____

_____

Design Your Own T-Shirt!

Judy took out a fat marker and drew a
big-mouthed shark with lots of teeth.
I ATE A SHARK, she wrote in all capitals.

Excerpt from *Judy Moody*

Now it's your turn to design your own
T-shirt! Fill in Judy's blank shirt with
something YOU would like to wear on
the first day of school.

Design Your Own Band-Aid!

Judy Moody is crazy for Crazy Strips!

"Rare!" Judy said. "I, Judy Moody, could have my own Crazy Strip."

Excerpt from *Judy Moody Saves the World!*

What design would YOU like to see on knees, ankles, and elbows everywhere?

Doctor Judy Moody Jokes

What does a skeleton take for a cold?
Coffin drops!

What do skeletons put on their mashed potatoes?
Grave-y!

What do you call a skeleton who sleeps all day?
Lazybones!

What does a skeleton eat for breakfast?
Scream of wheat!

What did the doctor say to the patient with tonsillitis?
Have a swell *time!*

When did Benjamin Franklin discover electricity?
During a brain *storm.*

What's the hardest kind of bow to tie?
An elbow.

What do kidneys say at the start of a baseball game?
Bladder up!

How long can you hold your breath?
A lung, lung time.

Why did Toady go to the hospital?
To get a hop-er-a-tion.

If you breathe oxygen all day, what do you breathe at night?
Nightrogen!

What did the right eye say to the left eye?
Just between you and me, something smells.

What falls asleep but never snores?
Your foot.

Where does a sick boat go?
To the dock.

What do you call an operation on a rabbit?
A hare cut.

Check out all the funny names for your bones!

face (cheekbone): zygoma
head: cranium
neck: cervical vertebrae
back: vertebral column
finger: phalange
arm: humerus
hip bones: ilium and ischium
leg (thigh): femur
knees: patellae
foot: metatarsus

Fill in the blanks with the funny-sounding names from George the Skeleton. (Answers at the back of the book.)

Pain in the <u>cervical vertebrae</u>

The bee's _____

Put your best _____ forward.

That's a _____ scratcher.

Red in the _____

Step on a crack, break your mother's _____

Costs a _____ and a _____

That's a _____ nail biter.

_____ , _____ , hooray!

Got a problem?
The doctor is IN.
Dr. Judy Moody,
that is!

Dear Judy,
My mom bought me new
shoes for school and they
rub! What should I do if I
have a blister?

Blister? DON'T pop it. Instead,
think of words that rhyme with
blister: mister, sister, kissed
her *(yee-uk!)*.
See? Now, didn't that make you
forget about your blister?
No? Then go play Twister.

Dear Judy,
I've got the hiccups!
How can I get rid of them?

Okay, which of the following is
NOT a cure for hiccups?
  a. standing on your head
  b. holding your breath
  c. eating a teaspoon of sugar
  d. blowing into a paper bag
  e. thinking of the color blue
  f. pinching your nose and
     drinking water
  g. jumping out of a plane
Tricked you! ALL of the above are
known cures for hiccups. No lie!

Dear Judy,
The lunch lady made me eat Brussels sprouts and now I feel sick. What should I do?

Okay, whatever you do, DON'T think of:
  a. worms
  b. slug slime
  c. ABC gum (Already Been Chewed)
  d. prunes
  e. toads
Better?
Oh well. I never said I was perfect.

Dear Judy,
Ow, I've got a headache!

When you have a plain, old-fashioned pain in your brain, you should ask your little brother to leave the room. You'll be amazed how fast your headache goes away! For sure and absolute positive! (If that doesn't work, try an ice pack.)

Dear Judy,
I have a frog in my throat! Any advice?

Absolutely.
You have three choices:
  a. Make it feel at home — swallow a tadpole.
  b. Open wide, say "ahh," and hope it hops out.
  c. Take two prunes and call your doctor in the morning.

The Phantom Doll Doctor Strikes Again

That's when Judy's brain began working on a brand-new Judy Moody idea.

She'd make a sign. Maybe set up shop in the garage. Get other kids to give her their broken dolls or old stuffed animals. Or she'd find some at yard sales. She would doctor them up and donate them to more sick kids in the Children's Wing at the hospital. Some could have Ace bandages, or fancy scars, or tubes for breathing. Maybe even an IV!

Excerpt from *Judy Moody Gets Famous!*

Help a sick kid in the hospital, just like Judy did! Here are some ideas to make kids feel better at a hospital near you:

- Write a letter to cheer somebody up.
- Make a get well card.
- Take them a teddy bear.
- Read a story.
- Make a cozy blanket to brighten up a hospital room.

Make a Fun and Fuzzy No-Sew Blanket! FOR REAL!

Make a cozy, warm blanket as a gift or for a needy kid. No sewing allowed!

1. At a fabric store, buy two different-colored pieces of polar fleece. The two pieces should be the same size, each slightly bigger than you want the final blanket to be. One handy size to try is a $1\frac{1}{2}$ x $1\frac{1}{2}$ yard square.

2. Spread one of the pieces of fleece flat on the floor, face-down. Lay the other piece directly on top of it, face-up, and line up the edges. You might want to pin the pieces together to keep them from shifting around. Trim any uneven edges.

3. Cutting through both layers with a pair of scissors, cut a 4-inch-by-4-inch square completely out of each corner.

4. Working your way around all four edges of the blanket, create a fringe with the scissors by making a 4-inch long cut every inch, again cutting through both layers of fleece.

5. Now it's time to join the top and bottom layers of fringe together. Starting at one corner, tie each 1-inch strip on the top layer to its matching strip on the bottom layer. Continue around the edges of the blanket until all the strips have been tied together. Remove any pins holding the layers together.

Voilà! Done!
It's that easy! No sewing!

Judy Moody Cootie Catcher

Moody? Broody? Or wriggly and giggly? Use the Judy Moody Cootie Catcher for some serious mood-acious advice!

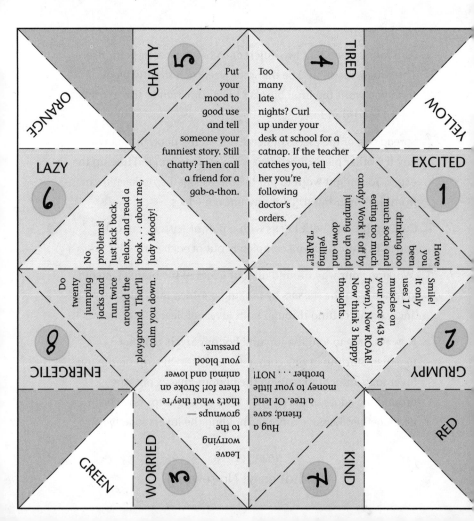

1. Photocopy and cut out the cootie catcher.

2. Printed side down, fold back all four corners to meet in the middle. Turn it over and do the same on the other side.

3. Fold it in half, with the color names facing out.

4. Now insert your thumbs and forefingers in the four square flaps, one in each flap, and hold them so they all meet at the center.

How To play:

1. Ask a friend to pick a color.

2. Spell out the color, opening the cootie catcher first one way, then the next for each letter.

3. Now get your friend to pick the word on the inside of the cootie catcher that best describes how he or she is feeling. Then count out the number beneath that word with the cootie catcher.

4. Ask your friend to choose a second word that best describes how he or she is feeling.

5. Now simply open the flap beneath that word for your Judy Moody mood advice!

Super Heroes and Heroines

Elizabeth Blackwell, First Woman Doctor

1821 Born in Bristol, England

1832 Comes to America

1847 After 28 rejections, is accepted to medical school

1849 Becomes first woman doctor, first in her class

1849 Moves to Paris, gets eye infection, loses vision in one eye

1853 Opens New York clinic for poor women and children

1854 Adopts Kitty Barry, a 7-year-old orphan from Ireland

1861 Trains nurses in the Civil War

1868 Opens first Women's Medical College

1876 Writes a book about children for parents

1910 Dies at the age of 89

Choose a person you admire.

Find out some facts about his or her life
and make a timeline:

Year: **Important event:**

_____   _____

_____   _____

_____   _____

_____   _____

_____   _____

_____   _____

_____   _____

_____   _____

_____   _____

Elizabeth Blackwell

Lived in an attic.
Nothing was automatic

First in her class
What more could you ask?

Became first woman doctor
Even though boys mocked her

Opened a clinic
Helped poor people in it

Delivered Babies
Gave shots for rabies (maybe)

Opened her own School
It was way cool

Wrote a book
Wonder how long it took

Born, I don't know when
Died, 1910

Take after the example
Of Dr. Elizabeth Blackwell

Excerpt from *Judy Moody, M.D.: The Doctor Is In!*

Write a poem about the person you most admire:

_____

_____

_____

_____

_____

_____

_____

_____

_____

_____

_____

Judy Moody

Have you read all of the Judy Moody books?

Title: Judy Moody

Date Read:

Comments:

Title: Judy Moody Gets Famous!

Date Read:

Comments:

Title: Judy Moody Saves the World!

Date Read:

Comments:

Reading Checklist

 Title: Judy Moody Predicts the Future

Date Read:

Comments:

 Title: Judy Moody, M.D.: The Doctor Is In!

Date Read:

Comments:

What ideas do you have for more Judy Moody adventures?

What other good books have you been reading lately?

Megan McDonald's favorite book when she was a kid was *Harriet the Spy* by Louise Fitzhugh. Peter H. Reynolds's favorite book when he was a kid was *Charlie and the Chocolate Factory* by Roald Dahl. What are your favorite books? List them here:

 Title:

Date Read:

Comments:

 Title:

Date Read:

Comments:

 Title:

Date Read:

Comments:

Magic, Mysterious
Ever-Changing Mood Rings!

Mood rings change color with your mood!
Make up a mood for each color on your mood ring:

Blue: _____

Green: _____

Red: _____

Amber: _____

Purple: _____

Black: _____

If your mood ring had extra special magic powers, what would you wish for it to do?

Draw a picture of your ESP (Extra Special Powers) ring.

Does your magic ring have a name?

Magic
8 Ball

Using the list of choices on the next page, what would you pick to answer each of these questions:

Will I get an A++ on my spelling test?

Will I eat a shark this summer?

Will I go to Disneyland?

Will I be president when I grow up?

Will I have a million dollars someday?

Will I dye my hair green?

Will I be a principal someday?

Will I write a book like *Judy Moody*?

* Signs point to yes.
* Yes.
* Reply hazy, try again.
* Without a doubt.
* My sources say no.
* As I see it, yes.
* You may rely on it.
* Concentrate and ask again.
* Outlook not so good.
* It is decidedly so.

* Better not tell you now.
* Very doubtful.
* Yes — definitely.
* It is certain.
* Cannot predict now.
* Most likely.
* Ask again later.
* My reply is no.
* Outlook good.
* Don't count on it.

Make up your own questions:

Will I _____ ?

Answer: _____

Will I _____ and live happily ever after?

Answer: _____

Will I ever _____?

Answer: _____

Will I _____ when I grow up?

Answer: _____

Judy tries some magic spells and potions to find out if Mr. Todd is really in love.

Bowl of water + Apple Seed + candle = true love

If you could make a magic potion, what would you want it to do?

Create your own recipe for a
magic potion here! Are there any
magic words that go along with
the potion?

_____

_____

_____

_____

_____

_____

_____

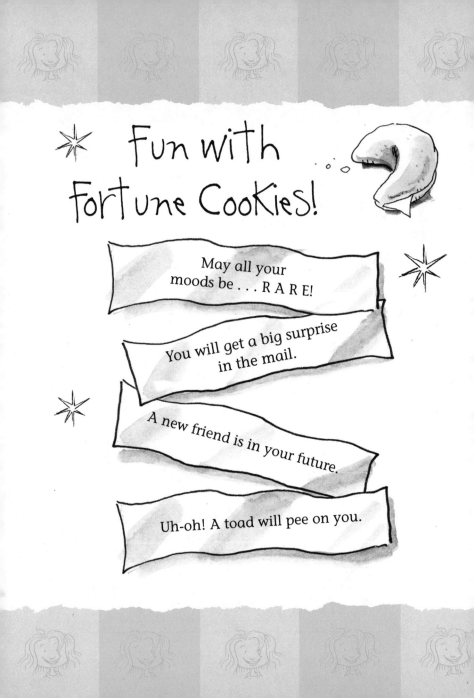

Fun with Fortune Cookies!

May all your
moods be . . . R A R E!

You will get a big surprise
in the mail.

A new friend is in your future.

Uh-oh! A toad will pee on you.

Make up your own fortunes!

Judy Moody
Crossword Puzzle

Across

2. Judy found one in a cereal box.
3. Name of piano-playing chicken
7. Name of Judy's club with friends
13. Name of Judy's teacher
14. Northeast beach tiger _____
15. Name of Judy's cat
16. What Judy ate one summer

Down

1. State where Judy lives
4. Judy's saying when happy
5. Nickname for Stink
6. Name of Judy's Venus flytrap
8. Judy collects these
9. Name of Judy's tree
10. Kind of pencil Judy uses
11. Mouse knows how to make this.
12. _____ Blackwell, first woman doctor

(Answers at the back of the book.)

Judy Moody's Declaration of Independence

with 7 alien rights

I, Judy Moody, do hereby declare:

1. Freedom from brushing my hair

2. Freedom from little brothers (as in Stink)

3. Freedom from baby bedtime (as in staying up later than Stink)

4. Freedom from homework

5. Freedom to have sleepovers

6. Freedom to have my own bathroom (and washcloth!)

7. Freedom to get pounds of allowance

Excerpt from *Judy Moody Declares Independence*

Do you ever feel like you need more independence?
Judy Moody does! Here's your chance to create your own
Declaration of Independence — complete with alien rights.

_____'s Declaration of
Independence with 7 alien rights

I, _____, do hereby declare:

1.

2.

3.

4.

5.

6.

7.

The Law of the Sugar Packets

Sometimes, the best advice can be found in unusual places!

A penny saved is a penny earned.

Don't cry over spilled milk.

Fish and visitors stink after three days.

And sometimes, it's better just to write your own advice, like Judy does!

A penny saved is never as much as Stink has.

Don't cry over spilled chocolate milk

Fish and little brothers stink after three days.

Now it's your turn!

What words of advice would you
like to see on a sugar packet?
Start your own sugar packet collection!

Secret Code

Judy's parents sent Judy on a treasure hunt around their house using this secret code. This code was really used to send secret messages during the American Revolution!

A = Z		**J** = Q		**S** = H
B = Y		**K** = P		**T** = G
C = X		**L** = O		**U** = F
D = W		**M** = N		**V** = E
E = V		**N** = M		**W** = D
F = U		**O** = L		**X** = C
G = T		**P** = K		**Y** = B
H = S		**Q** = J		**Z** = A
I = R		**R** = I		

Can you decode these messages from Judy?

1. QFWB NLLWB IFOVH!

2. LMV RU YB OZMW, GDL RU YB HVZ

3. KILFW NVNYVI LU GSV GLZW KVV XOFY

4. ILZI!

(Answers at the back of the book.)

Now try creating your
own messages for
your friends!

_____

_____

_____

_____

_____

_____

_____

_____

Test Your Judy Moody I.Q.

FOLLOW YOUR Star

WARNING: Even Judy Moody experts may be stumped! See how you rate in Judy Moody know-how. Check your answers at the back of the book.

Score (Number of correct answers)

1–6	**O**	**Oops!** Better read some more Judy Moody books!
7–12	**PG**	**Pretty Good.** Try sleeping with a Judy Moody book under your pillow.
13–18	**B**	**Brainiac.** You and Jessica Finch are Queen Bees.
19–24	**R**	**RARE!** You deserve a Thomas Jefferson tricorn-hat sticker.

EaSy

1. What does the T. P. in T. P. Club stand for?

2. What did Frank Pearl eat for a dare?

3. What saying was on Judy's Crazy Strip when she entered the Band-Aid contest?

4. Name one thing Judy Moody likes to collect.

5. Who is the T. P. Club mascot?

6. What part of Judy got into the newspaper when she entered the pet contest?

7. What did Stink have to do to get into the T. P. Club?

8. What was written on the T-shirt that Judy wore the first day of school?

Medium

1. What is Mr. Todd's nickname?

2. What famous person does Judy most admire and want to grow up to be like?

3. What is Mouse's famous pet trick?

4. What does Stink feed to Judy's Venus flytrap?

5. What does Judy do to try to get 100% on her spelling test?

6. What did Stink's Crazy Strip say?

7. What subject is Jessica Finch especially good at in school?

8. When Mr. Todd put on Judy's mood ring, what color did it turn?

9. What does the color purple mean on the mood ring?

Difficult

1. What does Judy call Jessica Finch?

2. What ice-cream shop does Judy like to go to?

3. What kind of pencil does Judy like to write with?

4. What name do they print (by mistake) in the newspaper for Judy Moody?

5. Judy finds an old school project in the trash when she tries to get her family to recycle. What is it?

6. What shape is the stain on Judy's "Me collage" when Stink spills grape juice on it?

SUPERDUPER EXTRA-SPECIAL BONUS QUESTION:

What song did the chicken play on the piano at the pet show?

Looking to the Future...

The future was out there, waiting. And there was one more thing Judy did know for sure and absolute positive — there would be many more moods to come.

Excerpt from *Judy Moody Predicts the Future*

If you had one wish for the future, what would it be?

What's your biggest dream?

Make a list of five goals that you would like to accomplish this year. Don't be afraid to think big!

1. _____

_____

2. _____

_____

3. _____

_____

4. _____

_____

5. _____

_____

✳ Birthday Book ✳

Keep track of all of your friends' birthdays here!

Name:	**Birthday:**
Judy	April 1

Throw a birthday party with a Judy Moody theme!

Here are some suggestions:

- Decorate using the colors from the Judy Moody book covers (green and orange for example).

- You may not have a Screamin' Mimi's near you, but you can still celebrate with ice cream! Get your favorite flavors and let everyone add their own toppings.

- Have a fortune-telling area with a Magic 8 Ball!

- Draw a big picture of Judy and play Stick-the-Band-Aid on Judy. Everyone wears blindfolds, and the person who sticks a Band-Aid closest to Judy's nose wins!

Print your name here:

Write your name in cursive here:

Doctors have messy autographs.
Sign your name like a doctor here:

Now sign it extra neatly:

Try writing with your left hand
(or right hand if you're a lefty!):

Want a real challenge? Try signing your name
with your foot here:

Get your friends to autograph your book here:

What famous person would you like to have
sign your book?

I like to be naughty.
I like to be nice.
But just to be moody
I'll sign my name twice.

Yours till Niagara Falls.
Yours till butter flies.
Yours till ——————— wear roller skates.
Yours till ——————— talk.
Yours till ———————.

Roses are ———————.
Violets are ———————.
Give me ——————— dollars.
And I will ———————.

Igpay Atinlay

Jessica Finch likes to speak in Pig Latin.

Judy Moody = Udyjay Oodymay

Stink = Inkstay

Rocky = Ockyray

Frank = Ankfray

Jessica Finch = Essicajay Inchfay

Toady = Oadytay

Mouse = Ousemay

Jaws = Awsjay

Sign your name in Pig Latin:

Get your friends to sign their names in Pig Latin:

What is your pet's name in Pig Latin?

✧ Judy Moody ✧

Read the book that started it all! Get to know Judy Moody through mad-faced moods, funniest-thing-ever moods, and every mood in between.

An American Library Association Notable Children's Book

A New York Public Library Best Children's Book: 100 Titles for Reading and Sharing

A *Publishers Weekly* Best Book of the Year

★ "The book itself has a look as fresh as its heroine. . . . The book opens . . . with a hilarious spread in pen-and-ink wash. . . . The dialogue is spot-on. . . . It's hard to imagine a mood Judy couldn't improve."
— ***Publishers Weekly*** (starred review)

"Judy is independent, feisty, and full of energy, a delightful new character for beginning chapter-book readers. Reynolds has captured her personality in his humorous illustrations done in watercolor, tea, and pen and ink."
— ***School Library Journal***

Judy Moody Gets Famous!

Judy Moody is in the mood to be a star. As each of her attempts to gain fame falls through, she hatches a new scheme, each one more outrageous than the last! One thing's for sure — after reading this, you'll be Judy Moody's biggest fan!

An ABC Children's Booksellers Choice

An American Library Association Notable Children's Book

An International Reading Association Children's Choices Award Winner

A *Children's Literature* Choice List Title

An Oppenheim Toy Portfolio Gold Seal Award Winner

★ "This sequel to *Judy Moody* handily matches the original in zip and wit. . . . Even Judy could spell two words that describe both the plot and its heroine: f-r-e-s-h and f-u-n-n-y."
— ***Publishers Weekly*** (starred review)

Judy Moody
SAVES THE WORLD!

Judy Moody is back, and she's in an environmental mood. Can Judy Moody come up with a plan to save the world?

A Book Sense 76 Selection

An International Reading Association Children's Choices Award Winner

A Chicago Public Library Best Book for Children and Teens

An Oppenheim Toy Portfolio Gold Seal Award Winner

★ "A delightful peek at a spunky third grader with a mood, and an idea, for every occasion. . . . Simple language, large print, lots of dialogue, and Peter Reynolds's quirky black-and-white illustrations only add to the kid appeal. . . . *Judy Moody Saves the World!* is cleverly written, and its heroine is an appealing and very real third grader." — ***The Five Owls*** (starred review)

Judy Moody Predicts the Future

When Judy Moody gets her very own mood ring, she decides to explore her psychic side, with unexpected and hilarious results. It's not hard to predict that Judy Moody's fortunetelling adventures will put you in a very, very good mood!

A Bank Street College Best Children's Book of the Year

"Established fans and new readers of the series will enjoy this adventure. Amusing black-and-white watercolors capture the humor and the girl's inimitable spirit. Prediction: another winner starring Judy Moody." — *School Library Journal*

"The irrepressible Judy is completely believable. . . . This is a great choice for first-chapter-book readers, especially those already acquainted with Judy." — *Booklist*

Judy Moody, M.D.
The Doctor Is In!

It's no secret that Judy wants to be like Elizabeth Blackwell, First Woman Doctor, when she grows up, so when Class 3T starts to study the Amazing Human Body, Judy can't wait to dive right in. This hilarious new episode is sure to tickle your *humerus* (AKA funny bone)!

"McDonald once again creates a feisty, individualistic, 'RARE!' third grader with a very active imagination, keen wit, and a strong desire to explore the world around her....This is another winner, 'for real and absolute positive.' "
— *School Library Journal*

"[McDonald] finds ample comedy in the way children mishear words and mangle information. Reynolds's buoyant sketches depict Judy's ups and downs in this fifth book of a series that proves laughter can be contagious." — *Booklist*

Judy's latest adventure!

Judy Moody Declares Independence
When Judy Moody's family takes a trip to Boston, Judy is inspired to declare independence. Will she be able to prove that she's ready for more freedom?

DOUBLE RARE!
Judy Moody has her own website!

www.judymoody.com

Check it out for the latest in all things Judy Moody, including answers to all your V.I.Q.'s about Judy, way-not-boring stuff about Megan McDonald and Peter H. Reynolds, and double-cool activities that will be sure to put you in a best-ever mood!

The Judy Moody Mood Journal

From the cool "Dial-a-Mood Meter" on the front to the fun prompts inside, this journal will get you in the mood to investigate — and celebrate — all the quirks and characteristics that make you unique.

The Judy Moody Star-Studded Collection

What's better than one Judy Moody adventure? The first three Judy Moody adventures — all packaged together in one instant paperback collection. Rare!

Catch Judy Moody's little brother in

Stink The Incredible Shrinking Kid

Judy Moody's brother, Stink, has always been shorter than she is . . . but now he worries that he might be growing even smaller. Could Stink be shrinking?

Megan McDonald ———

is the best-selling author of all of the Judy Moody books. "Sometimes I think I am Judy Moody," she says. "I'm certainly moody, like she is. Judy has a strong voice and always speaks up for herself. I like that." Megan McDonald and her husband live in Sebastopol, California, with a dog and fifteen wild turkeys that like to hang out on their back porch.

Peter H. Reynolds ———

is the illustrator of all of the Judy Moody books. He recalls that when he was approached about illustrating *Judy Moody,* he jumped at the chance. The feisty, independent Judy reminded him of his own daughter, who was eleven years old at the time. Peter H. Reynolds lives in Dedham, Massachusetts.

ANSWERS

Antidisestablishmentarianism: The belief that the tie between church and state should not be removed

Hippopotomonstrosesquipedalian: Having to do with a very long word!

ENDANGERED SPECIES:

northeast beach tiger beetle
   Cicindela dorsalis dorsalis
El Segundo blue butterfly
   Euphilotes battoides allyni
tooth cave spider
   Neoleptoneta myopica
shiny pigtoe
   Fusconaia cor
blunt-nosed leopard lizard
   Gambelia silus
Shenandoah salamander
   Plethodon shenandoah

BONE UP ON YOUR BONES

cervical vertebrae (neck)
patellae (knees)
metatarsus (foot)
cranium (head)
zygoma (face)
vertebral column (back)
humerus, femur (arm, leg)
phalange (finger)
ilium, ischium (hip, hip)

CROSSWORD PUZZLE

ACROSS
2. mood ring
3. Mozart
7. Toad Pee Club
13. Mr. Todd
14. beetle
15. Mouse
16. shark

DOWN
1. Virginia
4. rare
5. Stinkerbell
6. Jaws
8. Band-Aids
9. Luna Two
10. Grouchy
11. toast
12. Elizabeth

SECRET CODE

1. Judy Moody rules!
2. One if by land, two if by sea
3. Proud member of the Toad Pee Club
4. ROAR!

QUIZ

(Easy)

1. Toad Pee
2. paste
3. Heal the World
4. Band-Aids, scabs, pizza tables, spare doll parts
5. Toady
6. her elbow
7. have a toad pee on him
8. I ATE A SHARK

(Medium)

1. Mr. Toad
2. Elizabeth Blackwell
3. making toast
4. raw hamburger
5. sleep with the dictionary under her pillow
6. Batty for Band-Aids
7. spelling
8. red
9. Joyful, on top of the world

(Difficult)

1. Queen Bee or Jessica (Flunk) Finch or Jessica *Aardwolf* Finch or Jessica Fink
2. Screamin' Mimi's
3. Grouchy
4. Judy Muddy
5. her Laura Ingalls Wilder log cabin
6. Virginia

(Superduper Extra-Special Bonus Question)

"Three Blind Mice"

First edition 2005

ISBN 0-7636-2769-0

4 6 8 10 9 7 5 3

Printed in United States of America

This book was typeset in Stone Informal and Judy Moody.
The illustrations were done in watercolor, tea, and ink.

Candlewick Press
2067 Massachusetts Avenue
Cambridge, Massachusetts 02140

visit us at www.candlewick.com.

Dive right in and join the T.P. (Take out your Pencil) Club for hours of Judy Moody fun!

Get the lowdown on Screamin' Mimi's ice cream, prove your Judy Moody knowledge with quizzes and crosswords, make your own cootie catcher, and much, much, MUCH more! Whether you've just met Judy Moody or you're her biggest fan, this activity book is for you!

Warning: THIS BOOK MAY PUT YOU IN YOUR ALL-TIME BEST-EVER MOOD!

Check out www.judymoody.com
for the latest in all things Judy Moody!

Cover illustrations copyright © 2000 and 2002 by Peter H. Reynolds

$5.99 U.S.
$8.99 Canada
0605

www.candlewick.com

CANDLEWICK PRESS
2067 MASSACHUSETTS AVENUE
CAMBRIDGE, MASSACHUSETTS 02140

U.S. $5.99 / $8.99 CAN
ISBN 076362769-0

50599>

9 780763 627690

EAN